SIZZLE
PRESS

An imprint of Bonnier Publishing USA
251 Park Avenue South, New York, NY 10010

SIZZLE PRESS is a trademark of Bonnier Publishing USA, and
associated colophon is a trademark of Bonnier Publishing USA.
Manufactured in China HH 0617
First Edition 2 4 6 8 10 9 7 5 3 1
ISBN 978-1-4998-0656-4
sizzlepressbooks.com
bonnierpublishingusa.com

Under license by:
©2017 Moose Enterprise (INT) Pty Ltd. Grossery Gang™ logos,
names, and characters are licensed trademarks of Moose
Enterprise (INT) Pty Ltd.
29 Grange Road, Cheltenham, VIC 3192, Australia
www.moosetoys.com
info@moosetoys.com

contents

FOUL FOOD

You look like you're down in the dumps. What's eating you?
Worms, I think!

Q: What's worse than finding a worm in your apple?

A: Taking a bite and finding half a worm!

Q: What do you call a fruit that is rough around the edges?

A: A bad apple!

Q: What do you get if you cross an apple with a shellfish?

A: A crab apple!

Q: What do you get if you cross a Christmas tree with an apple?

A: A pineapple!

Q: What food do you get if you put a parakeet in the blender?
A: Shredded tweet!

Q: Why shouldn't you tell Rotten Egg a joke?
A: He might crack up!

Q: What's grosser than finding a slug in your hamburger?
A: Finding two slugs.

Q: What do you get if you eat too many onions and beans?
A: Tear gas.

Skummy Bear rushes past his friends, snatches up an apple, and gobbles it down, giving himself a bad tummy ache. He tells them that it's because he's heard that an apple a day keeps the doctor away.

"That's true," says Faulty Malty, "but you don't have an appointment with the doctor today. "

"I do now," replies Skummy Bear. "I've accidentally broken the doctor's window and he's chasing me!"

Shoccoli and Putrid Pizza walk into a coffee shop. Shoccoli orders a coffee and Putrid Pizza gets a tea. The owner refuses to serve them, and instead throws them out into the street.

"How many times have I told you both?" he shouts after them. "This is a coffee shop and we *don't* serve food."

Q: How do you make a milk shake?
A: You scare it!

Q: What did the gum say to the shoe?
A: I'm stuck on you!

Q: What goes "Snap, crackle, and pop?"
A: A fly landing on the barbecue.

Q: Why do the French eat snails, but the Americans don't?
A: Because Americans prefer fast food.

Q: What does a cat like to eat on its birthday?
A: Mice cream and cake!

Two frogs hop into their local takeout place. "Are you sure you've come to the right place?" the server asks. "There's nothing on our menu that frogs would like."

But the frogs disagree, scanning the menu. "French flies for me," says the first frog.

"And for me," says the second frog, "just a diet croak."

A customer was worried about getting fat, so he told his friend that he was going on a balanced diet. But the next day, he was munching on two huge hamburgers, one in each hand.

"I thought you were going on a balanced diet," said his friend.

"I am," the man replied. "The hamburger in my left hand balances exactly with the one in my right."

Scummy Soda went into a takeout joint and asked the server if he could make a special hamburger for him.

"I'd like the meat raw, the lettuce covered with flies, and the bun hard as a rock."

"That's gross," the server told him. "We can't do that."

"Why not?" asked Scummy Soda. "You did yesterday!"

Terrible Tomato Sauce and Squishy Tomato were walking down the street one day. Terrible Tomato Sauce was in a hurry to get to the Yucky Mart, but Squishy Tomato was walking too slow! So Terrible Tomato Sauce walked back to Squishy Tomato, jumped on top of him, squishing him into a red paste, and shouted, "Ketch up!"

Q: What do you call food that makes you run to the toilet?

A: Fast food.

Q: How do you stop a fish from smelling?

A: Cut off its nose.

Q: What do you often find in a rock-hard, stale donut?

A: Your teeth.

Q: What happened to the cannibal who was late for lunch?

A: He was given the cold shoulder.

Q: What happens if you step on a grape?

A: It lets out a little whine.

13

Barf-Room

Guess who my favorite superhero is.

Soap-er Man!

Puking Pumpkin walks into the bathroom and sees Shoccoli washing his hair with yucky brown stuff.

"Here, try some of my nice-smelling green shampoo," Puking Pumpkin says, picking up his own shampoo.

But Shoccoli sticks with the yucky brown stuff. "I don't like sham-poo," he says. "*Real poo* is so much better!"

Q: What did the bathtub say when he thought the toilet was sick?
A: You look flushed.

Q: Why did the toilet paper unroll down to the floor?
A: It wanted to get to the bottom of things.

Q: Why did the boy keep running to the bathroom at the party?
A: Because he was a party pooper!

Q: What's a tissue's favorite type of dance?
A: The boogie.

Fungus Fries bought 100 goldfish during a sale at the Yucky Mart.

"Where are you going to keep them all?" asked Horrid Hamburger.

"In the bathtub, of course," said Fungus Fries.

"But what will you do when you want to take a bath?" asked Horrid Hamburger.

"I'll blindfold them!"

Gooey Smooch is thirsty, so Sticky Soda kindly brings her a glass of water. She watches as Gooey Smooch drinks it in one gulp.

"Thank you, sweetie," Gooey Smooch says gratefully, shivering a little at the taste. Then she adds, "Look how tall you are! I didn't think you would be able to reach the kitchen tap."

"I can't," said Sticky Soda. "But I'm tall enough to reach the toilet."

Q: How many boys does it take to lift a toilet seat?

A: No one knows. They rarely bother to!

Q: How can you tell the difference between head lice and dandruff?

A: How they crunch in your teeth!

Q: What sort of cheese shouldn't you keep in the fridge?

A: Toenail cheese. Keep it in your toes!

Q: How do you keep flies out of the bathroom?

A: Flush the toilet!

Q: What did one piece of toilet paper say to the other?

A: I can't tear myself away from you.

19

Burp-rito entered a competition at the Yucky Mart, where the first place prize was a toilet and the last place prize was also a toilet.

"Why does the loser also win a toilet? asked Stinki.

"Because," said Burp-rito, "it's a win-loos situation."

In the bathroom, a toothbrush complains to its friend that he has a horrible job.

"I have to spend every morning and night cleaning gunk from people's teeth," he sighs.

"Don't expect me to feel sorry," says the friend. "I'm toilet paper!"

Q: Why is the boy with stinky toes good at running?
A: Because he has athlete's foot.

Q: Why did the superhero flush the toilet?
A: It was his duty.

Q: Why did the boy bring a bowling ball into the bathroom?
A: To watch his toilet bowl.

Q: Why can't you hear a pterodactyl go to the bathroom?
A: Its "p" is silent.

Q: Why did the robber take a bath?
A: Because he wanted to make a clean getaway.

Q: Why did the mummy go into the bath-room?
A: To wrap itself in toilet paper.

Q: What do you call a fairy using the toilet?
A: Stinker Bell.

Q: Why do skeletons never go to the bathroom?
A: Why would they? They don't have any guts.

Q: Did you hear the joke about the toilet?
A: Never mind, it's too dirty.

SiCK SCHOOL
How do you know if the egg you had for lunch at school was rotten?
You have n
friends in
the afternoo

Q: Where do cockroaches go to lose weight?
A: The school cafeteria.

Q: Why were the teacher's eyes crossed?
A: She couldn't control her pupils.

Q: What punishment can a school give that's worse than suspension?
A: Seconds for school lunches.

Chewed Candy and Fungus Fries were the only two people in class today. Fungus Fries asked Chewed Candy if he knew why. "Because you and I weren't here yesterday," said Chewed Candy, "but all the other kids were."

Fungus Fries frowned. He then asked Chewed Cand to explain further.

"Simple," said Chewed Candy. "We were the only ones who missed school lunch!"

When Shoccoli passed Smelly Bean's table, Smelly Bean couldn't help farting.

Shoccoli was very upset with him. "Smelly Bean!" he cried. "How dare you fart in front of me?"

Poor Smelly Bean felt really bad. "Sorry, Shoccoli," he said quietly. "I didn't know you wanted to fart first!"

Q: Why is it dangerous to have a food fight in the school cafeteria?

A: Someone might swallow the food!

Q: What's the good thing about lumpy school gravy?

A: It hides the rest of the food.

Q: How do you keep flies out of the school sauce?

A: Let them taste it.

Q: Why do school cafeterias often serve potatoes still wrapped in their skin?

A: Because the potatoes are always stone cold.

Q: What happens if you fart at school?

A: It gets expelled.

AWFUL Animal

Why do fish live in salt water?

Because pepper makes them sneeze!

SLIMY SARDINES

Q: What animal has four legs and one arm?
: A man-eating tiger.

Q: What do you call a flea that's crazy?
: A loony-tick.

Q: How do fleas get around?
: By itch-hiking.

Q: Why did the crow sit down in the middle of the road?
: To prove it had guts.

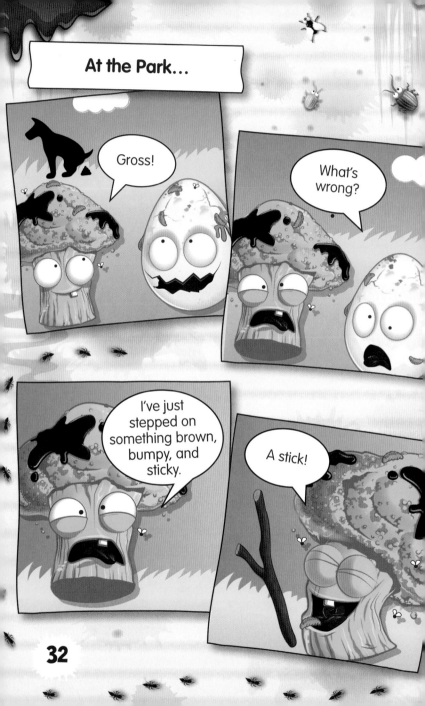

Q: What do you call a dinosaur in a car accident?

A: A tyrannosauraus wreck!

Q: What's every little skunk's favorite lesson at school?

A: Show and smell.

Q: What day of the week do fish hate?

A: Fry-day.

Q: How can you tell if a turkey farted?

A: The stuffing went all over the dinner table.

Q: What's the last thing that goes through a bug's mind when it hits a car's windshield?

A: Its butt!

33

A duck, a skunk, and a deer went out for dinner one night. When the waiter handed them the bill, he explained he had added an extra charge as the skunk smelled so bad that he had cleared out the restaurant.

"Well, I can't pay," said the smelly skunk. "I don't have a scent."

"And I can't pay," said the deer. "I don't have a buck."

So they had to put the meal on the duck's bill.

A baby mosquito flew away from home for the first time. When he came back home later, his father asked, "How was your trip?"

The baby mosquito replied, "It was great. Everyone was clapping for me!"

Krazy Kidz

Did you hear about the kidnapping at school?

It's okay. He woke up!

Dodgey Donut was making a cake for the Grossery Gang when Rotten Egg rushed in.

"Can I lick the bowl, please?" asked Rotten Egg excitedly.

"Only after you've finished flushing it," Dodgey Donut replied.

Cracked Cracker is at a party, sitting between Cruddy Chip and Barf Bagel. He loudly tells Cruddy Chip that he has to pee.

"You shouldn't use a word like that in public," replies Cruddy Chip. "Just say you need to whisper instead."

Cracked Cracker then turns to Barf Bagel, telling him he needs to whisper right away. The bagel leans toward him and says, "Okay, just do it quickly in my ear."

Q: What did the booger say to the kid's finger?
A: Stop picking on me!

Q: What's the difference between greens an green boogers?
A: Kids never eat their greens.

Q: Why do kids have two nostrils?
A: So they can pick their nose and breathe the same time!

Q: Why did Squished Banana peel?
A: Because he didn't wear any sunscreen!

Q: Why was it mean of Muck Muffin to tell Rancid Raisin Toast to be quiet or go play outside?
A: They were on a plane!

Q: Why was Icky Drumstick doing his homework while sitting on his hamster?

A: Because the teacher told him to write an essay on his pet!

Q: What time should Squishy Tomato go to the dentist to have his cavity filled?

A: At tooth-hurty.

Q: What's a pick-and-flick?

A: When you flick a booger.

Q: And what's a pick-and-stick?

A: When the booger is too gooey to flick!

Q: What's most kids' favorite bird?

A: Fried chicken.

Knock, knock!

Who's there?
Lettuce.
Lettuce who?
Lettuce in, it's cold outside!

Knock, knock!

Who's there?
Ice cream.
Ice cream who?
Ice cream every time
I see your face.

43

Knock, knock!

Who's there?
Amos.
Amos who?
A-mos-quito got stuck on my sticky bun.

Knock, knock!

Who's there?
Donut.
Donut who?
Donut talk with your mouth full!

Knock, knock!

Who's there?
Luke.
Luke who?
Luke at all that gross mold on your pizza!

Knock, knock!

Who's there?
Wanda.
Wanda who?
Wanda why you smell so bad!

Knock, knock!

Who's there?
Noah.
Noah who?
Noah where I left my booger?

Knock, knock!

Who's there?
Wooden shoe.
Wooden shoe who?
Wooden shoe like to hear another joke?